Pre-reader

Swim, Fish!

Explore the Coral Reef

Susan B. Neuman

NATIONAL
GEOGRAPHIC

Washington, D.C.

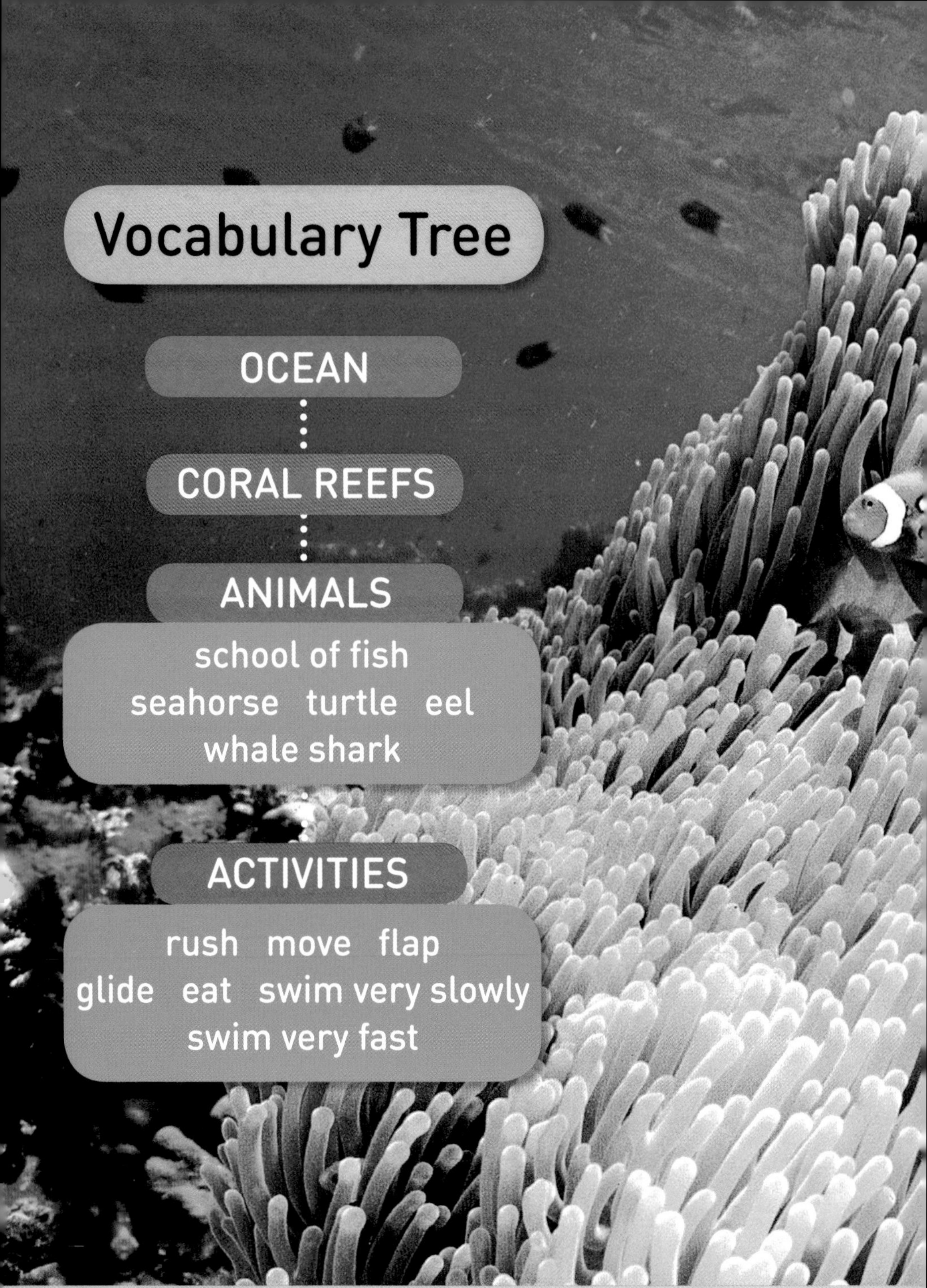

Vocabulary Tree

OCEAN

CORAL REEFS

ANIMALS

school of fish
seahorse   turtle   eel
whale shark

ACTIVITIES

rush   move   flap
glide   eat   swim very slowly
swim very fast

Let's swim!

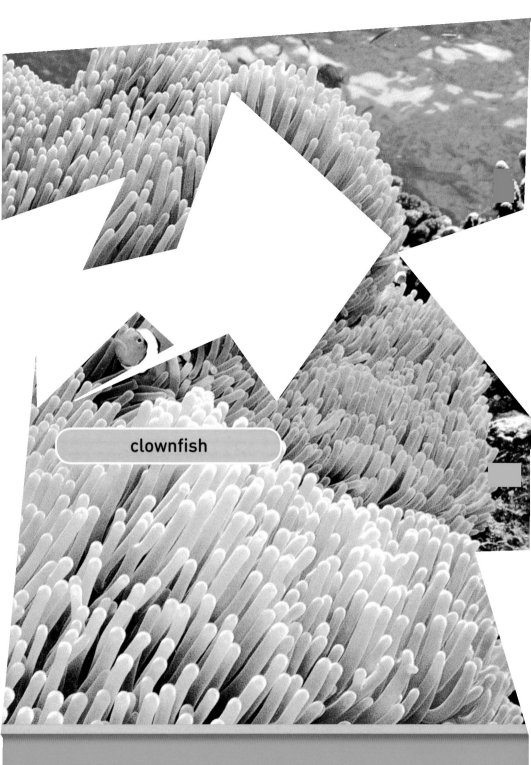

clownfish

Follow the fish to a coral reef.

The water here is warm.

Corals grow.
They make big reefs.

rush back and forth.

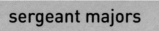

sergeant majors

seahorses

Seahorses move

up and down and sideways.

Turtles flap their flippers

green sea turtle

like birds flap their wings.

Eels glide from place to place.

giant moray eel

whale shark

Nearby, whale sharks

eat tiny fish.

Some animals here

cushion sea stars

swim very, very slowly.

Some swim very, very fast.

school of minnows

Swim, fish!

These animals live underwater.

The ocean is their home.

Coral Reef Map

Coral reefs are found all over the world. See where these animals live.

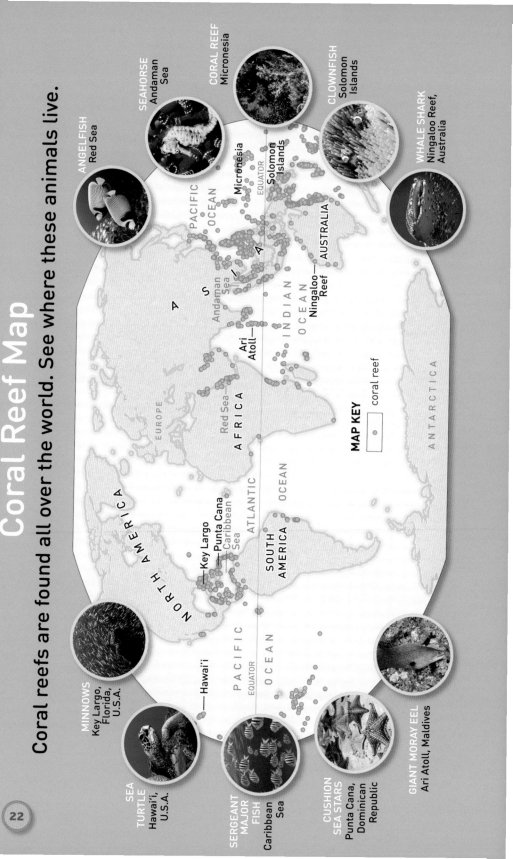

ANGELFISH Red Sea

SEAHORSE Andaman Sea

CORAL REEF Micronesia

CLOWNFISH Solomon Islands

WHALE SHARK Ningaloo Reef, Australia

MINNOWS Key Largo, Florida, U.S.A.

SEA TURTLE Hawai'i, U.S.A.

SERGEANT MAJOR FISH Caribbean Sea

CUSHION SEA STARS Punta Cana, Dominican Republic

GIANT MORAY EEL Ari Atoll, Maldives

NORTH AMERICA
SOUTH AMERICA
EUROPE
AFRICA
ASIA
AUSTRALIA
ANTARCTICA

PACIFIC OCEAN
ATLANTIC OCEAN
INDIAN OCEAN

EQUATOR

Hawai'i
Key Largo
Punta Cana
Caribbean Sea
Red Sea
Andaman Sea
Ari Atoll
Micronesia
Solomon Islands
Ningaloo Reef

MAP KEY
● coral reef

Which animals live in a coral reef?

The answer is on the next page.

Published by National Geographic Partners, LLC, Washington, DC 20036.

Book design by David M. Seager

Trade paperback ISBN: 978-1-4263-1510-7
Reinforced library binding ISBN: 978-1-4263-1511-4

Cover, Stephen Frink Collection/Alamy Stock Photo; 1, Georgette Douwma/Photographer's Choice RF/Getty Images; 2-3, Chris Newbert/Minden Pictures; 4-5, Georgette Douwma/Photographer's Choice RF/Getty Images; 6-7, Vilainecrevette/Shutterstock; 8-9, Georgette Douwma/Photographer's Choice RF/Getty Images; 10-11, David B. Fleetham/Blue Planet Archive; 12-13, Reinhard Dirscherl/WaterFrame RM/Getty Images; 14-15, Andy Rouse/npl/Minden Pictures; 16-17, Vilainecrevette/Shutterstock; 18-19, Off Axis Production/Shutterstock; 20-21, Brandon Cole; 22 (minnows), Off Axis Production/Shutterstock; 22 (sea turtle), David B. Fleetham/Blue Planet Archive; 22 (school of fish), Vilainecrevette/Shutterstock; 22 (sea stars), Vilainecrevette/Shutterstock; 22 (eel), Reinhard Dirscherl/WaterFrame RM/Getty Images; 22 (angelfish), Georgette Douwma/Photographer's Choice/Getty Images; 22 (seahorse), Georgette Douwma/Photographer's Choice RF/Getty Images; 22 (coral reef), Brandon Cole; 22 (clownfish), Gerald Nowak/StockImage/Getty Images; 22 (whale shark), Andy Rouse/npl/Minden Pictures; 23 (turtle), James D. Watt/Blue Planet Archive; 23 (angelfish), Georgette Douwma/Photographer's Choice/Getty Images; 23 (clownfish), Gerald Nowak/StockImage/Getty Images; 23 (puppy), AnetaPics/Shutterstock; 23 (bird), Nejron Photo/Shutterstock; 23 (orangutan), Kjersti Joergensen/Shutterstock; 23 (coral reef), Dudarev Mikhail/Shutterstock; 24, Birgitte Wilms/Minden Pictures

Printed in the United States of America
22/WOR/5

Did you find them all?